Women Come Alive Historic Women Pioneers Hall of Faith Photo Album

2007 100th Year Centennial Edition

Written & Complied By
Prophet Elijah L. Hill, MBA

All rights reserved. No. Portion of this book & pictures may be used without the written permission of the author, without written consent no portion of this book is to be used.

Copyright Pending @ May 2007 by Prophet Elijah L. Hill, with Library of Congress Washington, D.C.; printed in the United States of America.

Published by Perfecting the Kingdom International Ministries
Elijah L. Hill
P.O. Box 181937
Arlington, Texas 76096
hilsker@yahoo.com
For copies send an email to the above website, write the above mailing address, or call 214-636-7668.

1st National Supervisor Mother Lizzie Robinson 1911-1945

Omaha World-Herald
Wednesday, August 5, 1992

Council Says: Here's to You, Mrs. Robinson

BY JOE BRENNAN
WORLD-HERALD STAFF WRITER

Omaha's newest street name is Lizzie Robinson Avenue.

The City Council voted Tuesday to rename a three-block stretch of Erskine Street for the woman who helped organize the Church of God in Christ in Nebraska. The council approved the ordinance unanimously.

"Lizzie Robinson is significant historically for her role as organizer of the women's ministry for the church," said City Planning Director Gary Pryor.

Mrs. Robinson and her husband, Edward, started the first Nebraska congregation in Omaha in 1916. Both are deceased.

That was 10 years after she helped Bishop Charles Harrison Mason found the church in Lexington, Miss.

Erskine Street from 24th to 27th Streets will be renamed in honor of Mrs. Robinson. Among the supporters of the change were Pastor Elijah L. Hill, state historian for the church.

The predominantly black Church of God in Christ has 3.7 million members worldwide and is the second largest black church in the United States. The church has 16 congregations in Nebraska, including 13 in Omaha.

Robinson Memorial Church, 2318 N. 26th St., is named after the Robinsons. In June, the council designated the church and the former Robinson residence at 2864 Corby St. as historic landmarks. The designations were approved in February by the Landmarks Heritage Preservation Commission.

- Tax increases and job cuts draw fire at Omaha budget hearing. Page 23.
- Lottery and sales-tax money will help LaVista double its budget. Page 17.

The Presiding Bishop uncovered the significance of Mother Lizzie Robinson, and this inspired State Historian, Pastor Elijah Hill to have the secular world to acknowledge Mother Lizzie Robinson as significant to America's history by getting a street named after her, and having her daughter, Ida Baker's hom placed on the historic registry of historic places.

1912 Mother Lizzie Woods & her daughter Ida Woods the Mother daughter Evangelist team established the first all night prayer.

1932 L-R Mother Lizzie Robinson & Bishop C.H. Mason, Memphis, TN.

1913, Mother Lizzie Robinson walks from county line to county line setting up up Bible bands in every Church of God in Christ in the south.

1914, Pastor Edward D. Robinson was the husband of Mother Lizzie Robinson

1936, Memphis, TN, Right lower corner J.O. Patterson, Mother Lizzie Robinson, Bishop CH Mason & directly behind Mother Robinson is St. Samuel holding up a Bible, Bishop E.M. Page, Bishop William Roberts.

1945, L-R Secretary Mother Lillian Brooks-Coffey & Mother Lizzie Robinson in the pulpit in Memphis, TN.

1945, L-R Middle Mother Lizzie Robinson
Memphis, TN.

1945, Memphis, TN L-R Bishop Railey Williams, Bishop OT Jones, C.L. Morton, Bishop William Roberts, Mother Lizzie Robinson, Mother Lilliam Brooks-Coffey.

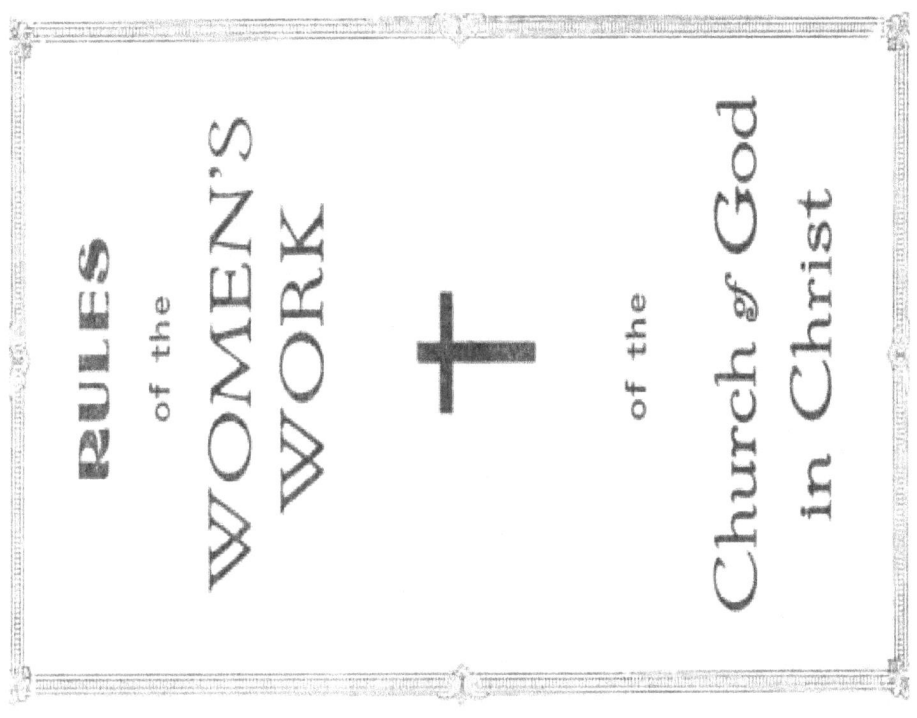

pastor and they will not be permitted to teach if it is fou'd out that she talks with the weaker ones of the church who fight the pastorship.

9 No sister who has two or three husbands unlawfully according to the doctrines of the church of God in Christ can be a Missionary.

10 Workers requesting some sister to work, send your request to your pastor or State Mother.

11 All sisters applying for License to do Missionary Work must come before the State Mother's Board with recommendations from their pastor.

12 These rules are to be read in Bible Board Meetings.

All members and all Missionaries in good and regular standing with the Church of God in Christ must work in unity with the State Overseer, State Mother and Pastor.

ELDER C. H. MASON, Senior Bishop
MOTHER LIZZIE ROBINSON
General Supervisor of Women's Work

1926

Mother Lizzie Robinson's first Rules developed for the Church of God in Christ Women.

1956 Omaha, Nebraska, Standing L-R Elder Robert Alexander, his mother, Deacon Archie F. Baker and ElderHalcom. Seated Mrs. Robert Alexander and children with Mother Ida Baker the only daughter of the late Mother Robinson. ☐ ☐

1944, Mother Lizzie Robinson's final project was to publish the first Women's Religious Magazine the Lifted Banner, which was in print for 36 years

Several remaining original copies of the LIfted Banner Magazine produced by the Women of the Church of God in Christ from 1944-1970's.

Phone W.E. 1376

11—10—1945

Mother Lizzie Robinson
General Supervisor of Women's Work
2723 North 28th Avenue
OMAHA 10, NEBRASKA

Bishop R. F. Williams national Chairman Holy greeting to you and the staff of Bishops at this meeting I am glad to tell you how glad I am to live to see our chief apostle year of Jubilee in this great Church of god in Christ when I Read Lev. 25:11 a Jubilee unto you we are glad Bishop Williams and you and others have stood up Exodus 17: 12—13. Bishop Need now to hold up his hand Moses 12th were they held his hands steady till the going of the sun I am glad Bishop Williams I thank for you and the staff Bishop and and pastor state Mother and Missionary I glad I am song I am and thus glad of the Unity of this great Church of god in Christ think of this old hymn, Blow ye the trumpet Blow. the gladly solemn sound let all the nations Know to Earth the Ransomed family, the the year of Jubilee has come the year of Jubilee has come Return ye Ransom Sinner home, ye Slave of Sin and Shame your Liberty at Jesus Redentive by his Blood through all the Earth proclaim the the year of Jubilee

1945, Mother Lizzie Robinson's Final Letter written to the National Church the year she died in Memphis, TN.

1945, Omaha, Nebraska Mother Lillian Brooks-Coffey purchased this gravestone on behalf of the National COGIC entitled Mother Lizzie Robinson 1860-1945, Organizer of the Women's Department of Church of God in Christ

Bishop Urges Church of God in Christ to Return to Roots

By Julia McCord
World-Herald Staff Writer

Ford ... "The Church of God in Christ has always been a church that believed in economic development."

The presiding bishop of the Church of God in Christ on Friday called on the church to go back to its roots in order to secure the future.

At a press conference at the Red Lion Inn, the Rev. Louis H. Ford of Chicago said Omaha is a key player in the effort.

"Omaha can do more to bring us back to where we want to go than any other city in America," Ford said. "That's because the (church's) roots are so deeply planted and woven together here."

Omaha was home to Lizzie Robinson, who Ford said was one of the church's "pioneering ladies."

In 1906 Mrs. Robinson helped the denomination's founder, Bishop Charles H. Mason, organize and structure the church. She was the first supervisor of women's auxiliaries.

From modest beginnings in Lexington, Miss., the Church of God in Christ has grown to 3.7 million members in 52 countries. But it has forgotten its traditional constituency, the disenfranchised, Ford said.

"What did our church specialize in back then?" he asked. "Grass roots people."

The church preaches a mix of pentacostalism and entrepreneurship, training its converts in the ways of business as well as in the ways of God.

"The Church of God in Christ has always been a church that believed in economic development," Ford said. "The church works from the top down (God) and from the bottom up (business)."

Ford came to Omaha for the 74th Annual Holy Convocation of the Nebraska Jurisdiction, which concludes today.

The northeast and eastern Nebraska jurisdictions recently merged because of the death of one bishop and the illness of another.

Ford said he had come to bring about unity "and begin the real growth with this state."

Bishop P.S. Brooks from Detroit was appointed interim bishop of the newly created jurisdiction in December and will serve until a permanent bishop can be named.

During the Great Depression, for example, the church taught people to farm, to sew, to run businesses. In Memphis, a black-owned bank financed farmers and other entrepreneurs when times got tough.

Today, Ford said, the church needs "to be the example for returning back to the roots of the real black church of America that lives for the people, by the people."

"We're going to stop turning our heads on the dope addicts, the prostitutes," he said. With a "little bit more love, a little bit more care," 90 percent can be brought to Christ, he said.

The church needs to open child care centers all across America, halfway houses and shelters in every large city and "get boys and girls to (the farm) to make them see livestock, let them plant fruit trees, teach them to be builders."

"Let's open some stores, stop marching and put the monies to working," he said.

Bishop Says Omaha Key To His Church

● Continued from Page 65

said. "That's what our church is all about."

In the spiritual arena, Ford said, the church also needs to get down to business. It needs to carry Jesus' message of salvation out into the streets.

"We still believe in all night prayer, asking, praying, clapping our hands and stomping our hands and so hearning," he said. "We will not run from our responsibilities in the community."

1991, Presiding Bishop Louis Henry Ford holds a press conference in Omaha, Nebraska, and reveals that Omaha, Nebraska historically is key to the National Church's history because Mother Lizzie Robinson helped the founding father Bishop Charles Harrison Mason establish our church through all night prayer meetings.

Omaha World-Herald
Wednesday, August 5, 1992

Council Says: Here's to You, Mrs. Robinson

BY JOE BRENNAN
WORLD-HERALD STAFF WRITER

Omaha's newest street name is Lizzie Robinson Avenue.

The City Council voted Tuesday to rename a three-block stretch of Erskine Street for the woman who helped organize the Church of God in Christ in Nebraska. The council approved the ordinance unanimously.

"Lizzie Robinson is significant historically for her role as organizer of the women's ministry for the church," said City Planning Director Gary Pryor.

Mrs. Robinson and her husband, Edward, started the first Nebraska congregation in Omaha in 1916. Both are deceased.

That was 10 years after she helped Bishop Charles Harrison Mason found the church in Lexington, Miss.

Erskine Street from 24th to 27th Streets will be renamed in honor of Mrs. Robinson. Among the supporters of the change were Pastor Elijah L. Hill, state historian for the church.

The predominantly black Church of God in Christ has 3.7 million members worldwide and is the second largest black church in the United States. The church has 16 congregations in Nebraska, including 13 in Omaha.

Robinson Memorial Church, 2318 N. 26th St., is named after the Robinsons. In June, the council designated the church and the former Robinson residence at 2864 Corby St. as historic landmarks. The designations were approved in February by the Landmarks Heritage Preservation Commission.

- Tax increases and job cuts draw fire at Omaha budget hearing. Page 23.
- Lottery and sales-tax money will help LaVista double its budget. Page 17.

The Presiding Bishop uncovered the significance of Mother Lizzie Robinson, and this inspired State Historian, Pastor Elijah Hill to have the secular world to acknowledge Mother Lizzie Robinson as significant to America's history by getting a street named after her, and having her daughter, Ida Baker's home placed on the historic registry of historic places.

Omaha World-Herald
Friday, August 21, 1992

Stretch of Erskine Now Lizzie Robinson Avenue

It is now official. A three-block stretch of Erskine Street, from 24th to 27th, also will be known as Lizzie Robinson Avenue. The street name recognizes the woman who helped organize the Church of God in Christ in Nebraska in 1916. The church has 16 congregations in Nebraska, including 13 in Omaha. Robinson Memorial Church at 2318 N. 26th St. is named for Mrs. Robinson and her husband, Edward. Both are deceased. Ennis Lipscomb, a City of Omaha employee, is pictured installing the new sign Friday morning.

Pastor Elijah Hill Historian of Nebraska organizes and impliments the first street naming for a women in Nebraska white or black.

1990, Chicago, Illnois L-R Pastor Robert Sander, Presiding Bishop Louis Henry Ford & Pastor Elijah Hill, istorian or Nebraska

1992, Omaha, Nebraska L-R Inaugural Banquet Presiding Bishop LH. Ford, Pastor Elijah Hill, Bishop Vernon Richardson, Pastor John Ford.

1947, Memphis, TN, Mother Lillian Brooks-Coffey becomes the Second National General Mother of the Church of God in Christ.

1951, California 1st Women's Convention L-R, Mother Mattie McGlothen and the second General Supervisor Mother Lillian Brooks-Coffey being picked up by limosine.

1951, California 1st Lillian Brooks-Coffey Special Train Ride L-R Bishop Samuel Crouch, 2nd General Supervior Lillian Brooks-Coffey, State Supervior Mary Davis, Standing behind Mother Coffey, Supervisor Anne Bailey.

1951, California 1st Women's Convention Pulpit shot L-R Bishop Charles H. Mason, 2nd General Supervisor Lillian Brooks-Coffey, Mary McLeod Bethune, Arenia Mallory

1946, Memphis, TN, 2nd General Supervisor's Inauguaral appointment, L-R, Mother Ida F. Baker daughter of the Late Mother Lizzie Robinson, the appointee the 2nd General Supervior Mother Lillian Brooks-Coffey, Bishop Railey F. Williams conducting Ceremony, behind is Mother Anne Bailey placing the cross of dedication around her neck.

1946, Memphis, TN COGIC World Headquarters L-R Mary McLeod Bethune & Second General Supervisor Mother Lillian Brooks-Coffey at her Installation Service as the 2nd General Mother of the Church of God in Christ.

**1946, Memphis, TN, World Headquarters Standing L-R
Unknown lady, 2nd General Supervisor of Women
Mother Lillian Brooks-Coffey, seated behind in the pulpit
Bishop Riley F. Williams, Mary McLeod Bethune.**

1951, California the Saints meeting 2nd General Superviors at the train Station for the Mother Lillian Brooks-Coffey Special. Standing L-R, Bishop SM Crouch, Mother Lillian Brooks-Coffey, Supervisor Mary Davis, Supervisor Hunter, Sister Anna B. Crocket-Ford.

1951, California first Women's Convention Banquet host Supervisor Mother Mattie McGlothen standing at podium, and sitting R-L Mother Ida F. Baker the Late Mother Lizzie Robinson's daughter, Mohter Anne Bailey, 2nd General Supervior Lillian Brooks Coffey.

WOMEN'S INTERNATIONAL CONVENTION 1956

SITE OF SECOND WOMEN'S CONVENTION

Bishop O. M. Kelley

—OUT NITE, NEW YORK, 1952—
China Town—Host and Hostess
Bishop & Mrs. Washington

The world is a looking glass, and gives every man a reflection of himself. We are happy that it is, and happier so we are happier to know that the Bishop & Mrs. Washington surely know that we will never forget the great reception given us that unforgettable night in New York, May 1952.

Mother Mayde Payton
State Supervisor

MT. MORRIS PRESBYTERIAN CHURCH
2 Mt. Morris Park   New York City, New York

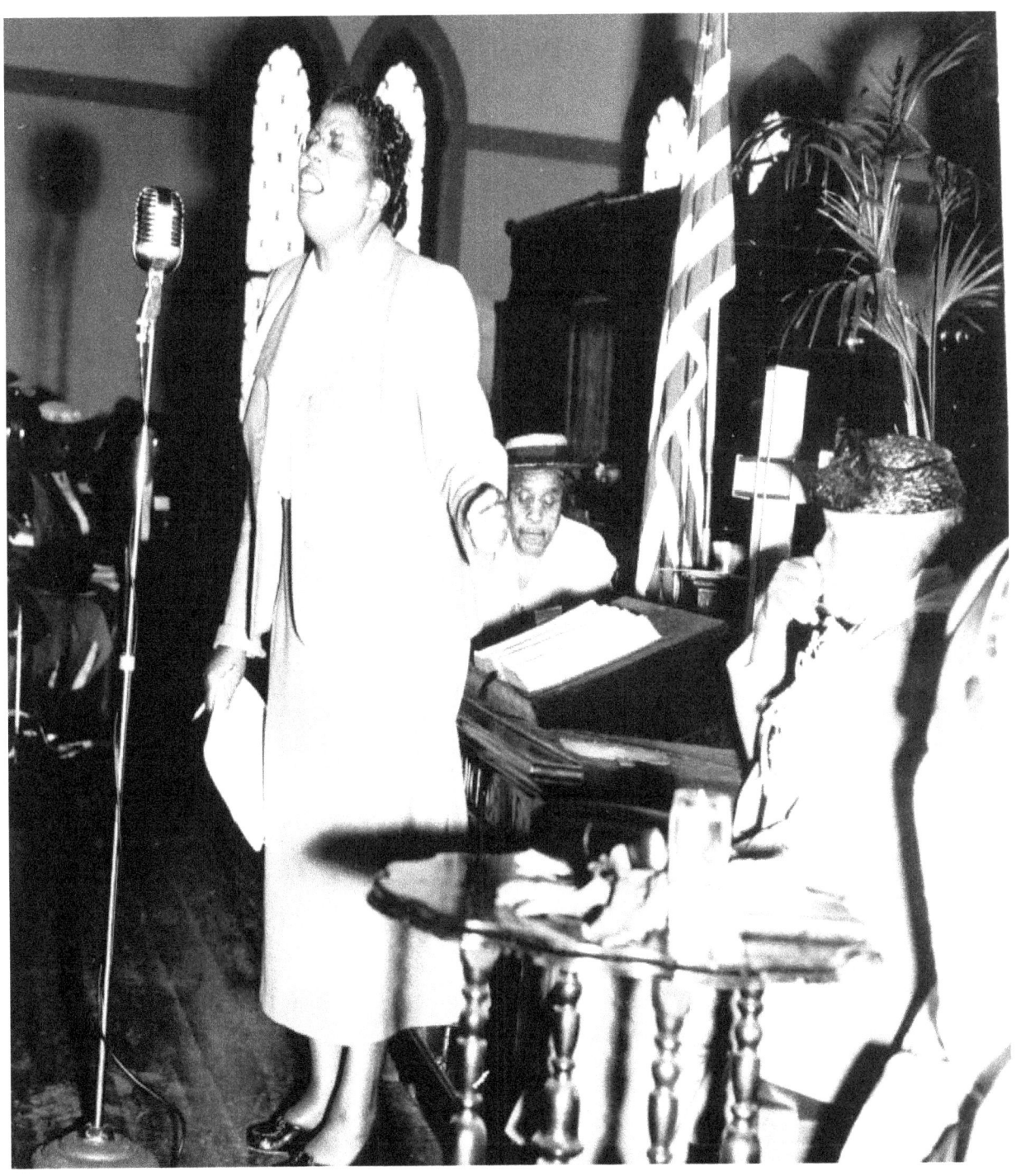

1952, 2nd Women;s Convention New York Women's Convention Ernestine Washington Singing a Solo for the Conventioneers.

3rd CONVENTION, MIAMI, FLA.

Bishop A. M. Cohen
Miami, Fla.

Mother Gussie Gamble
Fla.

Mass Meeting — Miami, Fla.

1953, Miami, Florida the 3rd Annual Women's Convention Host Bishop AM Cohen & Mother Gussie Gamble gathering in front of Bishop Cohen's Church.

SITE OF 4TH CONVENTION

ROBERTS' TEMPLE
4019-4021 State St., Chicago, Ill.

Pre-Musical—Chicago, Ill.

Concord Baptist Church
190 Warren Ave. — Boston, Mass.

Delegation Waiting To Be Taken On Motorcade.

1951, 1st Women's Convention San Francisco, California Group of Conven-tioneers posing. far left Supervisor Tenna Boone behind her Sister AnnaCrocket-Ford.

1951, 1st Annual Women's Convention, San Francisco, California L-R Front, Mother Mattie McGlothen, Unknown, Bishop SM Crouch, General Supervisor Lillian Brooks-Coffey, Supervisor Anne Bailey, Mother L.O. Hale, Behind L-R Debrorah Mason, Evangelist Retha Herndon, Supervisor Ida F. Baker, Supervisor Jennie Lou Hunter, Supervisor Mary Davis

— *Souvenir* —

International Women's Convention

CHURCH OF GOD IN CHRIST

MIAMI, FLORIDA

May 5th - 10th, 1953

Post Convention Trips

Cuba - Nassau - Jamaica - Haiti

1951, 1st Women's Convention pulpit shot 2nd General Supervisor & President of the Women's International Convention, seated L-R Mother Lillian Brooks-Coffey and Mary McLeod Bethune.

Lifted Banners

"He brought me into the banquet hall, and His Banner Over Me Was Love."

Lifted Banners

Synoptic Edition
NOVEMBER, 1953

A word fitly spoken is like apples of gold,
in pictures silver . . . Prov. 25-11

Lifted Banners

JANUARY, 1954

1958, Memphis, TN, working on the Lifted Banner Magazine, seated front General Supervisor Lillian Brooks-Coffey, Standing L-R, Supervisor Anne Bailey, Supervisor Ida F. Baker Mother Lizzie Robinson's daughter.

1965, the Four Big Wheels L-R, Supervisor L.O. Hale, Supervisor Anne Bailey, 2nd General Supervisor Lillian Brooks-Coffey, Dr. Arenia Mallory.

1955, Memphis, TN National Hospitality Women's Department seating in front of MasonTemple.

1965, Kansas City, Missouri Barker Temple COGIC, standing middle 2nd General Supervisor visiting Mother Lillian Brooks-Coffey.

1950, Memphis, TN, Seated L-R Mrs. Elsie Mason and Bishop Charles Harrison Mason, and standing behind J.O. Patterson.

1950, Elsie Mason's portrait

1955, Boston, MA, Standing L-R Bishop C.H. Mason, Mother Lillian Brooks-Coffey, Evangelist Letha Herndon, Bishop OT Jones Sr.

1951, Seated L-R, Mary McLeod Bethune & Dr. Arenia Mallory the National Council of Negro Women.

1955, Memphis, TN, Deborah Mason & Bishop CH. Mason

Pre-Convention Musical

HONORING

Lillian Brooks Coffee
PRESIDENT

Women's International Convention
CHURCH OF GOD IN CHRIST, INC.

Tuesday, May 7, 1957   **7:30 & 9:30 p.m.**
MICHIGAN STATE TEMPLE

3500 Elmwood Street   Detroit, Michigan

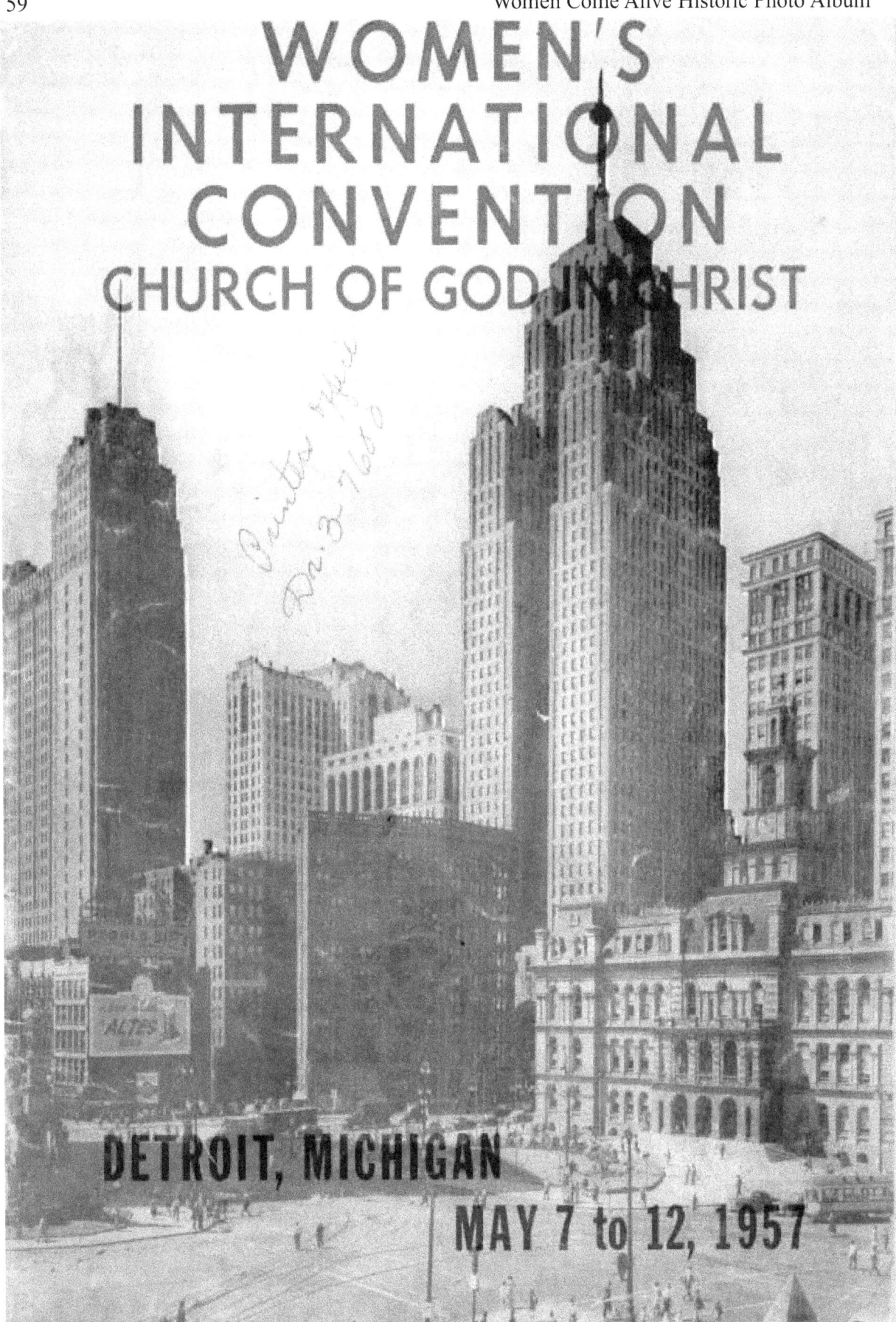

1951, Seated L-R, Mary McLeod Bethune & Dr. Arenia Mallory the National Council of Negro Women.

1955, Memphis, TN, Deborah Mason & Bishop CH. Mason

1951, 1st Women's Convention

1965, Mother Lillian Brooks-Coffey purchased the first jeep for Africa.

1965, Convocation in Memphis on Women's Day Foreign Delegates and missionaries from different parts of World.

**Missionary to Africa Elizabeth White
from 1930-1950**

Missionary Francina Wiggins to Africa 1949-56,

**Missionary Martha Barbour to Africa
1947-1955**

**Mother St. Justus Port Au Prince,
Haiti 1950-19670**

1965, Memphis, TN, L-R, Mother St. Justus, Bishop St. Justus Ports Au Prince, Haiti, Mr Bundany, India, Mother Lillian Brooks-Coffey, Bishop SM Crouch, .

1962, Convocation Foreign Missionaries from Africa in pulpit in Memphis, TN.

Missionary Dorthy Exume to Haiti

Missionary June Blackwell missonary to Africa

Missionary Elizabeth Scott, Nigeria, Africa, COGIC 1962-1969

**Missionary Pearl Page to Liberia West Coast
Africa 1969**

1951 1st Church Built in Africa

1955, Tubake, Africa, first girls dormitory built by Missionary Beatrice Lott of Dallas, TX

Missionary to Africa, Beatrice Lott, lays foundation for a Clinic, 1963.

**Missionary Beatrice Lott, of Dallas, TX,
Missionary to Africa 1937-1974.**

1962, Memphis, TN, Foreign Delegates from Africa standing with General Supervisor Lillian Brooks-Coffey.

First Orphanage built in Haiti, 1955, on porch L-R St. Justus and Missionary Dorothy Exhume.

Deborah Mason-Patterson Memphis, TN, 1963

Ella V. Sparks Editor of the Whole Truth 1924-1962.

Mother Elsia Shaw National Prayer Warrior COGIC

SISTER ANNA SMITH
General Recording Secretary

1918 Jessie R. Strickland, National Recording Secretary

**1950 Supervisor Mrs. Beulah Dabney,
National Prayer Warrior**

1955, Boston Motorcade L-R Bishop OM Kelly, Mother Lillian Brooks-Coffey, Bishop CW Williams, Bishop SM Crouch.

1955, Banquet Awards Group photo Mother Lillian Brooks-Coffey, Pastor U.E. Miller.

1950, Lydia Hinsley Editor of Sunshine Band Topics.

1955-1990 National Evangelist Rentha Herndon

1951, San Franciso, California Middle General Supervisor Lillian Brooks-Coffey, and Host Supervisor Mother Mattie McGlothen.

1950, Anna Crocket Chairperson National Women's Chorus Memphis, TN.

Ada Patrick, 1950-1965, National President of Purity

Allie Crutcher, 1950 National President of Young Women's Christian Council

**1950 Cora Berry, National Theology Institute
Chair Memphis, TN Morning Session**

1950, National President of the Overseers Wives Circle, Ada Taylor

1951, Bishop C.H. Mason in pulpit at 1st Women's Convention.

1951, 1st General Supervisor of Women Mother Lillian Brooks-Coffey in pulpit giving directions for Convention.

1955, Memphis, TN Convocation Blind Evangelist Draines chairwomen of the Handicap Unit

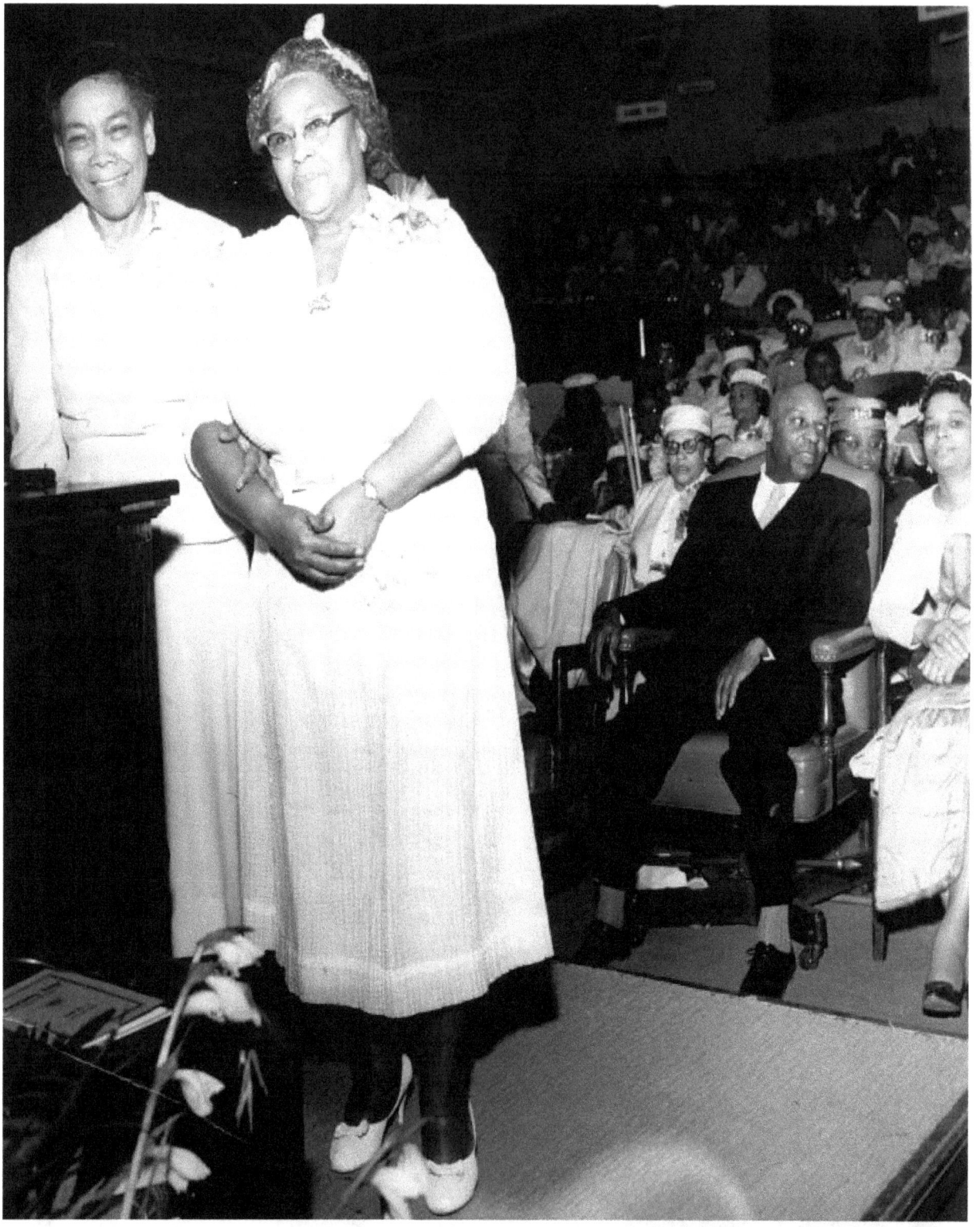

1963, Memphis, TN National Holy Convocation General Supervisor Lillian Brooks-Coffey introducing Mother Anne Bailey, and seated in background Bishop SM Crouch & Deborah Mason-Patterson.

1951, Bishop Charles Harrison Mason validating 1st Banner March

1950"s Governor of California meetings COGIC President of the Women's Convention L-R Governor & wife Mother Lillian Brooks-Coffey, unknown, Supervisor Mary Davis, Chicago, Supervisor Jennie Hunter, Chicago

1950, L-R 2nd General Supervisor of the COGIC Women's Department Lillian Brooks-Coffey hold flag with foreign missionary

1955, Awards given from, L-R front Genral Supervisor Mother Lillian Brooks-Coffey, Bishop U.E. Miller

1951, San Francisco, California, 2nd General Supervisor displaying first banner march during 1st COGIC Women's Convention

1955, Women's Convention Govenor'sMansion, L-R, Supervisor Mary Davis, 2nd General Supervisor Lillian Brooks-Coffey, Supervsor Jennie Hunter

1950, brainstorming session Memphis, TN, for the Women's International Convention

1955, Supervisor Ira Cotton, established first COGIC church in Alaska

WOMEN'S DAY

National Convocation
Church of God
in Christ

December 8, 1964

Her Alpha:
    Mother Ann Bailey

1960, 3rd General Supervisor of the Women's Department Mother Anne Bailey

**1943, Earlier picture of 3rd General Supervisor
Annie Bailey**

**1963, Mother Lillian Brooks-Coffey introduces
Mother Annie Bailey as her successor in Memphis, TN**

1946, Memphis,TN 2nd General Supervisor's Installation Service, L-R, Mother Annie Bailey places cross of dedication, 2nd General Supervisor Mother Lillian Brooks-Coffey, Bishop Riley F. Williams performs Service

1951, 1st Women's Convention Banquet the Host Supervisor Mother Mattie McGlotthen addresses conventioneers

19th Annual Women's Convention

of the
Church of God in Christ

May 6-11, 1969   Dallas, Texas

1966, Memphis, TN, L-R, 3rd General Suprervisor Mother Annie Bailey & Mother Ida F. Baker daughter of the late 1st General Supervisor Mother Lizzie Robinson

1966, Women's Convention Ribbon cutting Ceremony standing middle 3rd General Supervisor cutting ribbon

Women's International Convention

Church of God in Christ

Story in Pictures
1970
Oklahoma

"It's The method that changes not the principle."

21st Annual Women's Convention of the Church of God in Christ

MAY 18–23, 1971
Detroit, Michigan

"LEST SOME FORGET AND OTHERS NEVER KNOW"

CLIMBING THE LADDER OF SUCCESS—SPANNING TROUBLED WATERS AND CLOUDS OF OBSCURITY

PIONEER WOMEN
OF THE CHURCH OF GOD IN CHRIST

Silver Anniversary

the
International Women's Convention
of the
Church of God in Christ, Inc.

May 20-25, 1975
San Francisco, California

Dr. Anne L. Bailey, President

1966, Memphis, TN, Women's Department Meeting, L-R seated 3rd General Supervisor Annie Bailey, Supervisor Ida F. Baker, unknown, Supervisor Mattie McGlotthen

1966, Memphis, TN, Women's Department Meeting

Supervisor Cara Gardener 1969

Supervisor Elizebeth Hampton, Washington, DC, 1969

Supervisor Eloise Franklin 1969, Springfield, Mass

Supervisor Emma Mason, Kansas East 1969

Supervisor Fannie Becks, North Mississippi, 1969

Supervisor Hannah Bell, Southern Ohio, 1969

Supervisor J.V. Boyd, Colorado 1969

Supervisor J.V. Hearne, Oklahoma, NorthWest, 1969

Supervisor Katie Frasier, Georgia, 1969

Supervisor Margie Key, Maine & Rhode Island, 1969

Supervisor Mary Hopkins, Michigan, 1969

Supervsior Sweetie Porter, Nevada, 1969

Supervisor A.B. Jones, Iowa #1, 1969

Supervisor Alberta Jennings, Utah, 1969

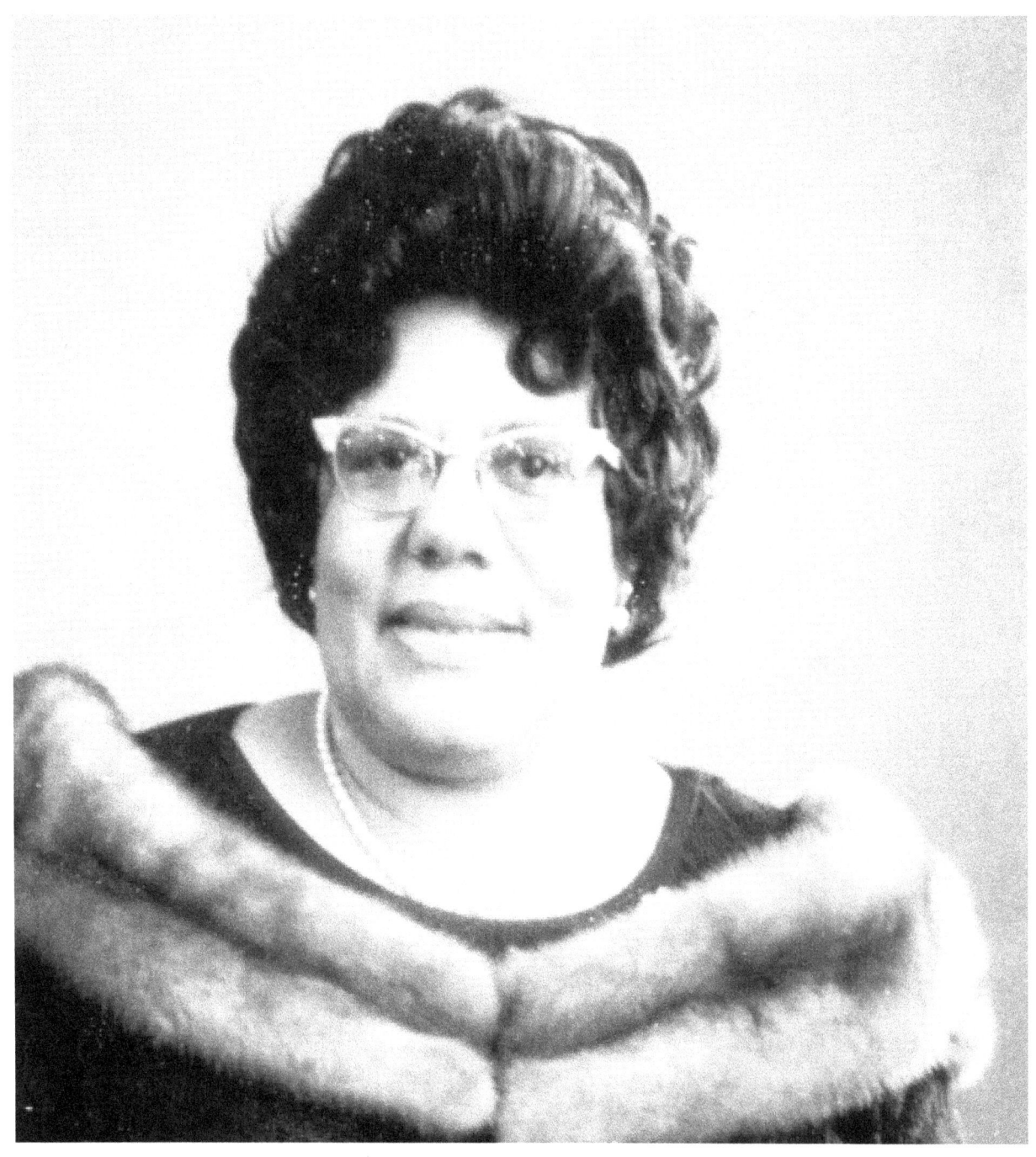

Supervisor Beulah Hatchett, Indiana North, 1969

Supervisor C.L. Buchanan, South Mississippi, 1969

**Supervisor Alberta McKenzie, Nebraska,
Editor of Lifted Banner, 1969**

Supervisor Corine Roberson, Texas Big Three, 1969

Supervisor D.S. Norris, Western, LA, 1969

Supervisor E.M. Devers, Northenrn, California, 1969

Supervisor E.M. Majors, Eastern Shore, Maryland, 1969

Supervisor Elizabeth McGill, Des Moines, Iowa # 2, 1969

1969, Supervisor Joan Price, New Mexico

1969, Supervisor Buford, Minnesota

1969, Supervisor Carrie Cantrell, Illinois

1955, Supervisor Hollis, East St. Louis, Illinois

1969, Supervisor Nebraska Ida F. Baker, daughter of the Late 1st General Supervisor

1969, The Fourth General Supervisor of COGIC

1969, Mother Willie Mae Rivers, North Carolinia

1914, 1st Supervisor Hanna Chandler of Texas

1969, Supervisor Elsie Kane West

**1945, Supervisor Emma Benson,
Iowa**

1945, Supervisor Lula Williams, Southeastern, Oklahoma

1945, Supervisor Willie Holt, Honolulu, Hawai

1945, Supervsior Bobbie Buffins, Minnesota

1945, Supervisor Costroma Sim, Winconsin

1945, Supervisor Emma Chambers, Northern Indiana

1945, Supervisor CA McFarland, Idaho

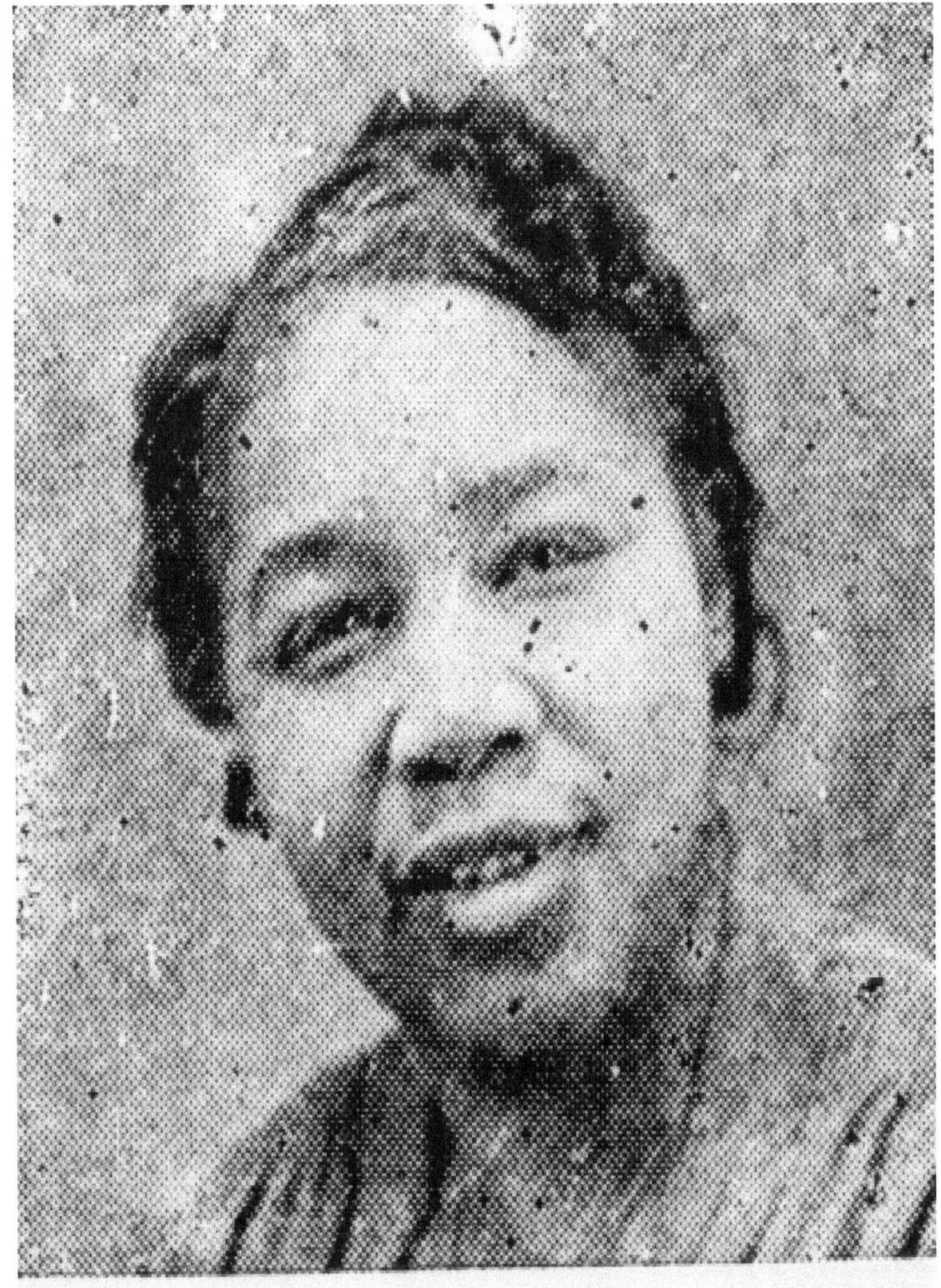

1945, Supervisor Jessie Ford, Southern Dakota

1945, Supervsior Lola Corrbitt-Young, Ohio

1965, Supervisor Emma F. Barron, Texas NorthEast

1969, Supervisor Emma F. Crouch, Texas Southwest

1945, Supervisor EL Jones, Utah

1945, Supervisor, D.M. Matthews, Connecticut

1969, Supervsor Esterlene Odom, Western Missouri

1969, Supervisor Fannie Mann, Virginia # 3

1969, Supervisor Fannie Page, Tennessee # 2

1969, Supervisor Georgia Burton, Delaware

1955, Supervisor Gussie Gamble, Florida

1969, Supervisor of Hampton, VA

1969, Supervisor Lydia Hinsley, Atlanta, Georgia

1969, Supervisor Ida Martin, Western Pennsylvania

1969, Supervisor Ira Lee Cotton, Alaska

1969, Supervisor J.L. Glover, Upper Manhattan, NY

1955, Supervisor Jennie Lou Hunter, Illinois & Chair of the National Volunteer Department.

1969, Supervisor J.M. McCants, North Carolinia # 1

1967, Supervisor Jessie Ford, Southeast Illinois

1969, Supervisor Jessie B. Washington, South West, Arkansas

1969, Leceola Anderson, West Corda, British Columbia

1969, Supervisor Lola Young, Cleveland, Ohio

1969, Supervisor Lorene Netter, Alabama # 2

1969, Supervisor Lossie M. Crear, Oregon

1969, Supervisor Louella Butler, Nebraska

1969, Supervisor Lovie E. Range, East Pennsylvania

1969, Supervisor Lula Little, Rhode Island

1969, Supervisor Luxola Williams, Nebraska

1969, Supervisor Mable Houston, Texas

1969, Supervisor Mattie Byars, Kansas

1969, Supervisor Mary Davis, Chicago, Illnois

1969, Supervisor Minnie M. Dowthard, Montana

1969, Supervisor Mytle Brooks, Texas

1969, Supervisor Nanie Penn, New Jersey

1969, Supervisor Norene Evans, Hawaii

1969, Supervisor Ola Garner, Arizona

1969, Supervisor Rebekah E. Gorham, Connecticut

1969, Supervisor Rosie Hines, Central Illnois, # 2

1969, Supervisor Ruthie Mae Shivers, Jackson, Mississippi

www.ingramcontent.com/pod-product-compliance
Lightning Source LLC
Chambersburg PA
CBHW081224170426
43198CB00017B/2708